MW00514216

Renewal

Also by Sharon Merz:

Strength for the Body & Soul
31 Recipes, Readings & Reflections

Renewal

A Spiritual Journey

By
Sharon Merz

Renewal: A Spiritual Journey
© 2023 by Sharon Merz
All rights reserved.

Unless otherwise indicated, all Scriptures in this book are quoted from The Holy Bible, New International Version ®, NIV ®. Copyright © 1973, 1978, 1984, 2011 by Biblica, Inc. ® Used by permission. All rights reserved worldwide.

Scripture quotations marked CEV are taken from the Contemporary English Version, copyright © 1995 by American Bible Society.

Scripture quotations marked NLT are taken from the Holy Bible, New Living Translation, copyright © 1996, 2004, 2015 by Tyndale House Foundation. Used by permission of Tyndale House Publishers, Inc., Carol Stream, Illinois 60188. All rights reserved.

Scripture quotations marked ESV are taken from the Holy Bible, English Standard Version. ESV ® Text Edition: 2016. Copyright © 2001 by Crossway Bibles, a publishing ministry of Good News Publishers.

Library of Congress Control Number: 2023916177

ISBN: 978-1-957497-29-7

Printed in the United States of America.

Cover photo by Vicky Pannella.
Design by Heather Lipe, Woodchuck Arts.

Dedication

This book is dedicated to Stephanie Johanpeter, whose prayers and sound advice helped start me on my path toward "Renewal."

Sadly, she passed away as this book was being finished, but her lively spirit continued to drive me toward completion.

It is my prayer that at least one person reading this book will find the same "renewal" that I have thanks to the wisdom of "Pastor Jo."

Proverbs 11:30:

"The fruit of the righteous is a tree of life, and the one who is wise saves lives."

Proverbs 13:14:

"The teaching of the wise is a fountain of life, turning a person from the snares of death."

Table of Contents

Renewal poem

Part II - Preparing for the Journey

"Just a Closer Walk With Thee"

Part III - The Beginning of Your Journey

"Do not be conformed to this world, but be transformed by the renewal of your mind, that by testing you may discern what is the will of God, what is good and acceptable and perfect."

Romans 12:2
English Standard Version

Introduction

Have you ever heard the caveat, "be careful what you say on Facebook"?

This book is black-and-white proof of that.

Three large states currently separate me from my friend Doug Apple. But we are close because of some "life overlap" that often puts us on the same page.

Oddly enough, we've never met in person. However, Doug grew up in the "little town" where I later lived as an adult. We both attended the same university and earned Journalism degrees just one year apart, although his focus was in radio broadcasting and mine was in newspapers and printing.

We both enjoy writing Bible-based devotions, so we have connected in a way that most people wouldn't understand. Writers tend to look at things differently, so Doug and I understand somewhat how each other's brains work. Because of these "coincidences," it's natural for us to comment on each other's Facebook posts.

Like that one day.

Doug actually records his excellent devotions because they air on the Christian radio station which he manages, but he posts the script as well as the audio link to "My Heart is on Fire" on his Facebook page. One particular day, his devotion included an exhortation that his readers and / or listeners develop the habit of a regular quiet time.

I couldn't resist.

"A regular quiet time has certainly changed my life and strengthened my faith! I would be happy to help anyone who's not sure about the logistics or how to get started! (I've actually led seminars because I'm so passionate about it!)"

In typical Doug fashion, he replied, "Sharon, have you written about it? You've got me curious!"

Knowing I had already started down a slippery slope that I wasn't sure was wanted, I hedged slightly. "I have a little. My former church in town here became involved in discipleship growth, and a regular quiet time that includes responding to God's word was the cornerstone. A 'devotional life seminar' was a regular offering and I was highly involved."

I continued, "Studies have shown a regular quiet time to be the most significant factor in spiritual growth."

Doug prodded, "Maybe it's time to write up your story and personal testimony and your tips into one tidy little devotional!"

We switched to private messaging to continue the conversation, and "Renewal" is the result of that exchange.

I confess that my "personal testimony" wasn't something I looked forward to sharing. Indeed, even writing about the pain and anxiety was uncomfortable to me at times, even though the actual experiences were more than a decade ago.

Doug gave me those much-needed pushes as I was starting the process. There is no doubt in my mind that Doug Apple is remarkably skilled in both writing and encouraging!

1 Thessalonians 5:11: "Therefore encourage one another and build each other up, just as in fact you are doing."

I now encourage you to
begin your own
spiritual journey toward
"Renewal."

Part 1

The Beginning of <u>My</u> Journey

Chapter 1

High Anxiety

January 30, 2011: A date which will live in infamy.

No, my history isn't that bad. I fully realize that for most people, December 7, 1941, is "a date which will live in infamy" as President Theodore Roosevelt referred to the bombing of Pearl Harbor that propelled the United States into World War II.

January 30, 2011: A date which will live in infamy.

No, my history isn't that bad. I fully realize that for most people, December 7, 1941 is "a date which will live in infamy," as President Theodore Roosevelt referred to the bombing of Pearl Harbor that propelled the United States into World War II.

January 30, 2011 holds a great deal of significance for me because it's when I was guided in a way that rerouted me to spiritual maturity. It was a day in which I was filled with a lot of anxiety, but two kind and godly women helped to put me on a new path that, over time, has brought genuine renewal to my life.

But I want to back up a bit to put my life at that time into context—how it was that a person who isn't good at asking for help realized I desperately needed to do just that.

In August 2009, I moved to a moderately small town from a cozy little town in the Midwest. They were only 25 miles apart, but I had started working in the small town while living in the little town.

My life in the little town was getting increasingly stressful. Many consider living in a close-knit community with a modest population to be idyllic. While it certainly can be, there are still some of the same problems that exist everywhere. And while the house where my family lived was in a highly visible location, no one would guess that what went on behind closed doors was nowhere near idyllic.

A marriage filled with verbal and mental abuse was taking an untold toll on me internally. "Untold" is appropriate because I am such a private person that it took several years of abuse before I even shared the strife with my best friend. Taking walks and talking with her was the only time I could truly be myself. But all along, I just kept hoping and praying that things would get better. They never did.

That obviously frustrated me on many levels. At one point during that tumultuous time, I was teaching a women's Bible study. One of my lessons was about putting God between yourself and your problems. I wasn't really grasping that, so I had pretty much decided to just conveniently gloss over it during the lesson. In typically intrusive fashion, our house cat decided to plop its body on my workbook while I was studying on the couch.

That's when I got it.

When the cat put himself between me and the book, my focus switched to the family feline. It all made perfect sense: putting God between myself and my problems would put my focus where it should have been all the time: on the Almighty One. I shared that with the ladies, and for several years, I would often be reminded of that illustration by one of those who had been in the class that night.

Praying is one way to invite God to stand between yourself and a problem, but as the pain mounted in the depths of my soul, my attention was definitely on the difficulty, and my prayers couldn't seem to shift my focus.

Those who live with people who have bipolar disorder are subject to the ups and downs that characterize the condition. I'm sure everyone responds differently; I tended to camp out in the valley while struggling not to be consumed by the actual and potential problems it was creating in our house.

Coming home was always a guessing game: will he be up or down today? As I would drive home from work every day, the tightness in my chest never failed to take me by surprise. But I knew it wouldn't do any good to see a doctor about it – there was no doubt in my mind that my anxiety was at such a high level that it was causing symptoms that felt like a heart attack. No amount of deep breathing, praying, or using music to distract my mind seemed to help.

As stressful as it was to think about stepping back into the house, actually being inside was worse. A home is supposed to be a refuge, but for me, it was a place where I was constantly "walking on eggshells." There was no way of knowing what comment or look would be perceived as an attack, which would result in a verbal assault on my character or mind, spewing from his mouth like venom from a snake. His paranoia only added to the turmoil.

Things that most people would say help the condition, like medication and counseling, didn't. It made the situation worse for me, as the blame for having to do those things was placed squarely on my shoulders. It seemed like everything was my fault, and that repeated assertion made me believe it.

Behind the smiles that I used to greet people at work, church, and around town, I felt myself as a person fading away. Visiting friends out of town to try and clear my head, one of them commented that I reminded her of a dish cloth that had been wrung out so intensely that it was nearly dry – devoid of its previous vitality.

The accuracy of my friend's description startled me. I felt totally drained of everything – except anxiety.

But I didn't know what to do about it.

Chapter 2

A New Chapter

The decision to leave the 21-year marriage after about a decade of decline was a very difficult one.

At that time, only a handful of people knew what my home life was really like. I had finally reached out to my pastor. I guess I was hoping he would have some profound, biblical advice that would turn things around. But part of me also wanted to be able to stop making excuses for why my husband was rarely at church anymore.

No profound advice came other than to make sure I would have a safe place to go if things escalated to physical abuse. I had always denied to myself that was a possibility, but hearing someone else mention it just raised the anxiety to another level. My last sliver of optimism had been shredded.

And things just kept getting worse. And worse. And worse. I understand now that it was only by the grace and strength of God that I was able to function despite all of the effects the anxiety was having on me.

I preached to myself:

> *"Cast all your anxiety on him because he cares for you."* 1 Peter 5:7

> *"Do not be anxious about anything, but in every situation, by prayer and petition, with thanksgiving, present your requests to God."* Philippians 4:6

I was praying a lot. These verses assured me of God's care and interest, but the continual barrage of unexpected attacks kept me in a constant state of anxiety.

We were in the car one day, and he asked if I wanted to stop and see a certain friend. When I said I didn't, his anger seethed against me–even though he didn't want to see her and especially didn't want to see her husband. It was just one more example of the inconsistencies that characterized him and shredded the fabric of what was left of our marriage.

It was time to start planning my departure from him, and staying in the little town didn't seem like the smart, or safe, thing to do. Moving to the small town where I worked seemed like a logical choice. The logic of it didn't cancel the fact that it was also frightening and nerve-wracking; the anxiety moved with me.

A new town also meant a new church. My first visit involved me sitting with my head lowered and tears flowing for most of the time. My attempts at hiding and blending in weren't completely successful because the pastor's wife approached me during greeting time and asked if she could sit with me. At the end of the service, she didn't pry but could tell I was scared, so she asked if I was safe. I told her I was, but I wasn't completely sure of it myself.

I decided to return the following week. And the next. It was good to feel like God had led me to this church when I wasn't sure that I was still in His favor for leaving the marriage. I had neglected to praise Him for all the many ways my departure plans came together. I knew the Lord still loved me but doubted if He would ever let me be of service to Him again.

But the church literally and figuratively embraced me. It was a long process, of course, but it seemed like a labor of love for them. The members basically loved me into a position of healing, freely sharing themselves and the assurance of God's desire to use me once again for His glory. The church itself had no qualms about me serving; the condemnation I had been feeling for so long had been replaced by loving grace.

I finally felt at home and started to relax and find myself again.

As time went on, I was able to make cherished

friendships, and we would socialize inside of church and outside those walls as well. I was welcomed into their lives and homes. I experienced genuine affection from people who simply accepted me for who I was, with no regard for the guilt and anxiety I had brought to church with me. They prayed for me and with me. Healing started to occur, and God began to renew my strength as promised in Isaiah 40:29-31:

He gives strength to the weary and increases the power of the weak. Even youths grow tired and weary, and young men stumble and fall; but those who hope in the LORD will renew their strength. They will soar on wings like eagles; they will run and not grow weary, they will walk and not be faint.

How I was so blessed to be at that church! I was surprised at how easily I adjusted to a larger building and congregation.

With a larger attendance, my new church home had two Sunday morning services, with Sunday school classes sandwiched in between. A couple of friends would sometimes attend the early service, go to Sunday school, and then attend a small sister church in the country just a few miles north of town.

On January 30, 2011, that's what my friend Sue and I did as feelings of being overwhelmed were mounting, and my anxiety was returning as new problems surfaced.

Chapter 3

The Front Pew of the Country Church

While I had come a long way in healing from the wounds acquired in my marriage, there were some things in my life that were changing, so my life was far from being trouble-free.

My new church was a blessing in numerous ways. I had found a nice place to live in a quiet neighborhood. But there were some situations that fueled my tendency toward anxiety.

My job was increasingly stressful and demanding. I was starting to develop some perplexing health issues for the first time in my life. A close relationship in my life was also proving challenging.

The pastor of the country church was a compassionate woman. The ministry was a second career, as she had worked as a nurse for many years. In my mind, she was the perfect person for me to talk with about my multiple anxiety-producing situations. I was comforted when my friend, Sue, agreed to go with me to the country church after services at our home church.

The drive to the church was only about 10 minutes. It was a sunny January day, and the plain white church with the bell tower looked like a postcard against the clear blue sky. With no more than 20 pews, the laid-back setting was a good fit for Stephanie Johanpeter to serve as pastor of this small congregation.

More commonly known as "Pastor Jo," she was approached by several of those in attendance following that morning's sermon. Having to wait for an opportunity to speak privately with her did nothing to dispel my anxiety.

Sue had retired from the local school system and is very sweet and easy-going. She had been to the country church many times, so she knew everyone there. Knowing the heavy burden I carried, Sue patiently kept talking to me while we waited for "my turn."

When the small church began clearing out, I approached Pastor Jo to ask if I could share a few things with her. A compassionate woman with the true heart of a servant, she led me to the front pew in the church, and we sat down to talk.

I started with my health issues. She was genuinely concerned, mentioned a few things that could be the cause, and then instructed me to make an appointment with my doctor to get thoroughly checked out.

I then moved on to the relationship issue. Since Pastor Jo also knew the friend, she was able to share some insights and encouraged me to keep praying and let God figure things out.

Then it was her turn to ask me a question: "How's

your spiritual life right now?"

I admitted that it was feeling a little sluggish, so Pastor Jo asked if I did a quiet time. I told her that I had tried to develop that practice over the years but hadn't been able to stick with it.

"Do you have one of my 'God Jobs' bookmarks?" she asked. When I shook my head, Pastor Jo asked Sue to bring me a bookmark from the back of the church.

"God Jobs" is just another name for spiritual disciplines, she explained, adding that the term was coined by a theology professor, Robert Mulholland.

Pastor Jo had created the simple bookmark, which lists inward disciplines, outward disciplines, and together disciplines on the front. On the back are the instructions for "The Deep Read" for meaningful Bible reading and meditation. She suggested I give it a try.

More than twelve years later, I'm still doing "The Deep Read." It's a practice that has helped me to grow to the point that it literally changed my life and brought the renewal that I desperately needed.

"The Deep Read" has numerous virtues that make it a vital tool in my spiritual life. I'll go into extensive detail in Part Two, but for now, I'll just say that Pastor Jo's advised that I use it to approach the Bible just a few verses at a time and respond as I felt led by the Holy Spirit. Those are the instructions for "The Deep Read" in a nutshell – it's just that simple.

Just a few minutes on the front pew of a country church marked what I consider to be the beginning of much-needed renewal in my journey of spiritual maturity.

By the time Sue and I left, I was feeling better already.

Chapter 4

Beyond Reading

In short, "The Deep Read" is a method in which the person reads a short passage of Scripture, then meditates on it to inspire some sort of personal response.

My previous idea of a quiet time or devotion time was basically just reading the Bible. And, of course, the larger the Bible passage, the better! "The Deep Read," like other similar methods designed to foster spiritual development, takes believers beyond reading.

I'm a morning person (yes, one of those people who honestly doesn't mind getting up when it's still dark out), so I've always done my quiet time in the mornings. So, on January 31, 2011, the morning after my front-pew counseling session, I went beyond reading the Bible to "deep reading" it.

Making notations in an ordinary composition book, here is how I responded the first week to the various Scripture passages after meditation:

- Muddy waters are no match for God, who will always allow me to stand firm on dry ground (Joshua 3:17)
- God will guide me through whatever happens, so I'll be okay. (Philippians 1:27)
- I asked myself, "what do I need to devote to the Lord?" (Joshua 6:17)
- Great joy and comfort come from knowing someone understands you. (Isaiah 40:28)
- I need to stop being surprised at the way non-believers treat me. (1 John 3:13)
- Man-made barriers are no match for God. (John 20:26)
- No matter how much I fail, God never does. (Joshua 21:45)

Sometimes encouraging. Sometimes convicting. Sometimes prompting praise. Sometimes motivating me to examine myself. Always an insightful start to my day so my focus is on God right out of the gate.

I confess that I often take on new "things" with great excitement but quickly lose interest. I'm no stranger to vigorous efforts to develop good habits to improve myself in some fashion—diet, exercise, new hobbies, etc. They don't seem to last. The luster fades, and boredom sets in. Goodbye, good intentions.

So, I was admittedly a bit surprised when that didn't happen with my new quiet time routine. I began approaching my time with the Lord with great anticipation. I was excited about how each day seemed fresh with insights!

This was clearly a different way to approach not only the Bible but also God. I increasingly sensed that humility was really the only way to approach God and felt that being developed as I spent just a few minutes every morning in my quiet time.

About six weeks into my quiet time, God showed me something that has become HUGE in my spiritual walk. The insight was so profound and so impactful that I just had to share it.

Chapter 5

"Amazing Things"

About six weeks into doing the "Deep Read" on March 11, 2011, God truly showed me "amazing things."

That was the morning I read what has become one of my favorite verses:

> *"Consecrate yourselves, for ... the Lord will do amazing things among you." (Joshua 3:5)*

With the death of Moses, Joshua became the leader of the Hebrew nation, which had just finished 40 years of wilderness-wandering due to disobedience and unbelief. The new generation was preparing to finally enter the Promised Land, and Joshua had them all gathered to give them a pep talk before crossing the Jordan River.

His message: Get ready, because God's gonna knock your socks off!

But I noticed something else in that message that really spoke to me: the people had to consecrate themselves for God to do "amazing things among" them.

God was ready to wow them, but only if THEY were ready.

Consecration is an act of preparation for holiness. It takes a tremendous amount of humility, but the Lord makes it all worth it.

My personal responsibility to humbly submit myself so God could do "amazing things" in my life is what hit me like a ton of bricks that morning. "Am I prepared for the Lord to do amazing things?" is what I wrote in my notebook.

It was a weighty question. I really wasn't sure of the answer, either. Was it possible that hanging onto my anxiety was holding me back from what my heavenly Father wanted to accomplish in my life? Joshua 3:5 became the focus of my prayers as my soul longingly searched for the answer.

The timing of the discovery of this impactful verse was incredible as well. At the time, I was the secretary of a board at church, and the board's chairman and vice chairman were coming to my home that night for a planning overview of the next meeting. I jotted in my notebook that "this seems appropriate to pray that God would prepare us – and we would prepare ourselves for amazing things."

After discussing the business for the upcoming meeting, I shared Joshua 3:5 with Ray and Rex. They both agreed that it was a fitting verse, and I was gratified to have the encouragement from my good friends.

Shortly afterward, I got a message from Rex. He had also been profoundly impacted by the verse. He felt we should use it to challenge the church members to be more focused on the throne of God so that He could do "amazing things" in the church and those in attendance. The focus was on humility and worship.

Rex wrote in a proposal to the committee, "The leadership … strongly believes in the (throne) challenge and the promise of Joshua 3:5. We also believe that in this very pivotal time at the church, it is important that as many people as possible join us as we consecrate ourselves and bring everything before the throne of Christ. This is the key to the spiritual growth of the church; therefore, we feel the [leadership] should first be challenged to begin thinking in the ways spelled out. We then would like to challenge the Church Council and then extend it out to the rest of the church."

We shared it with our Sunday school class. We shared it with the choir. A few others became as excited about "amazing things" as Rex and I had become.

It was all about humility. It was all about focusing on God. It was all about spiritual maturity and renewal.

All because I spent a few minutes reading five Bible

verses and meditating on them.

That's what I call "amazing things!"

Chapter 6

On the Move, Part 1

As I continued doing the "Deep Read," I could sense God's moving in my life.

I accepted Jesus Christ as my personal Lord and Savior at the age of 9. Since I started my spiritual journey, I began maturing.

Sermons, Sunday school classes, small groups, prayer, reading the Bible and Bible-based literature, and even music have all been part of my growth over the years.

And when I neglected those things, it stunted my growth.

When I was a child, my family didn't attend church, so my exposure to God was mainly comprised of hearing the Lord's name used in vain and the prayer before eating at the annual family reunion.

We were living on 23 acres when a neighbor, who

was also the leader of my Brownie Scout troop, asked my parents if they would allow her to take my older sister and me to church with her. My parents consented, so we started going to church with Marilyn. It was the same place where our Brownie meetings were held, so the setting was comfortable for me, even though I had never been to church before. I enjoyed the new experience of music and learning new things, and the acceptance I felt there was far different from any other part of my life.

Shy and very reserved, I was always well-behaved and a good student. I loved learning, and when I realized being a "good kid" would never get me to Heaven, I got on my knees.

The adults at church nurtured my spiritual journey, and I continued to love being at church more than anywhere else. About three years after my conversion to Christianity, I was crushed to learn that I would have to leave church because we were moving to a different town.

Some of the kids in the new neighborhood attended the same church and invited me to Vacation Bible School the summer we moved into our new home. While that was an okay experience, I realized the new church wasn't the same as my old one. Since my parents never attended church, it didn't matter to them one way or the other if I did. Not feeling the same connection in the new church, I stopped attending.

Then a couple of years later, we moved again as I started high school. With all the things to learn and the extracurricular activities that drew my interest, church never crossed my mind.

Then there was college, not exactly an environment that was spiritual in any way. I didn't get involved in all the heavy partying, but God, the Bible, and church continued to be nothing more than a part of my past.

Adult life was full of burdens. I got a job right out of college in my degree field of journalism. The little town was a good fit for me, as I enjoyed doing community journalism and getting a variety of experience in print production as well as a lot of writing.

Despite that, something was missing. I just couldn't put my finger on it.

One day while watching a football game, I noticed someone in the stands holding a banner that said, "John 3:16." I immediately recognized that as a well-known Bible verse that I had memorized as a child but couldn't remember a word of it at that point in my life. I dug around and found my Bible with its turned-up corners, something I apparently thought I should keep even though it was just taking up space at the bottom of the hall closet.

I found John 3:16 and read it. And remembered.

I remembered how much I was accepted at church,

not just by God but by the congregation. I remembered how I had experienced support at church that I didn't have at that point in my life. I remembered that I felt most whole when I was attending a church that kept me plugged into God.

God was calling me back to Him.

Chapter 7

On the Move, Part 2

I didn't answer right away, despite acknowledging that part of the emptiness I was feeling was probably because I had disconnected from God.

A few months after I was re-introduced to John 3:16 and that worn Bible, a friend extended an invitation. She knew I was struggling with some things, and she offered to let me come along one weekend as she visited her parents, who lived a few hours away. She let me know upfront that they would be attending church on Sunday morning.

So, I went. As a few tears fell from my bowed head and dotted my dress, I prayed for the first time in probably a decade, simply acknowledging that I needed God in my life that I had managed to mess up.

When my friend and I returned to the little town, I began attending church with her. I later discovered another church was a better fit for me, and it was there that I was finally baptized at the age of 25.

I grew a lot at that church, and that's where I met the man who would eventually become my husband, the father of my child—and my abuser.

After more than 21 years of marriage, I left the little town and moved to the small town.

I had moved a lot in my life, but I never liked it. Moving is a lot of work, but more than that, I never enjoyed the uncertainty each new location presented. I'm actually a big fan of security and stability; moving never seemed to include any of that.

But God does!

Your home, car, job, church, and family may change, but God never does. "Jesus Christ is the same yesterday and today and forever" (Hebrews 13:8). That's just one reason why I love the Lord!

Through the "Deep Read," I came to know and love the Lord even more. The more time I spend communing with God using that devotional method, the more I came to learn not only about His character but also how much my Creator loves me and how much He wants for me. I realized God alone could provide me with the security and stability I craved. Meditating on those types of things in small, manageable doses, my confidence in myself grew right along with my faith.

It was such a gradual process of renewal that I hardly noticed. But others did.

Especially after "the call."

Chapter 8

On the Move, Part 3

I had loosely been job searching for a couple of years, having posted my resume on an internet website. Each time I was slightly interested in a job, I would apply and pray a simple prayer: "Your will be done." As God continued to show me the importance of humility, that was how I felt led to pray.

One morning, the email listing featured a job doing pretty much what I was already doing. I submitted my resume, exchanged a couple of emails with the company's Human Resources Manager, then did a phone call, which led to an in-person interview with a few tests. A week after sending my resume, I called the HR Manager to ask a couple of questions, and she offered me the job. Wow!!

The only problem was that it was in a major metropolitan area, still in the Midwest but not in the same state where I had lived my entire adult life.

The job was appealing on so many levels, but this

small-town girl does NOT like big cities. And this one was two states away from my wonderful church.

As much as I hated the thought, I knew God was telling me to move. Again.

Many at the church marveled at the transformation in me in the less than three years I had been there. One woman commented, "Three years ago, you wouldn't have been strong enough to do something like this." She was right. The Lord had used many people and many things to get me to the place where I was able to move away to a big city, despite knowing virtually no one there.

Several people asked me, "Aren't you afraid of making a move like this all by yourself?" The only answer I could give was this: "God is going with me; I'm not doing this alone."

If someone had told me in January of 2011 that all this would transpire, I wouldn't have believed them. I wouldn't have believed in my ability to do it. But that was before God brought renewal to my life.

By the way, that move to the big city worked out very well. The job and the company were as wonderful as I had hoped they would be. An added bonus is that I met this guy, one whose life reflects his love for God and models servanthood. So, we got married (even though that meant ANOTHER move!) That was certainly an "amazing thing" I never saw coming as I prayed about moving to the big city.

I know I still have a long way to go in my spiritual maturity. I admit that my anxiety demon still comes knocking, and sometimes I open the door just enough that it's too much. But I have a better foundation for dealing with that and many more challenges that life on this earth brings.

God is always on the move, and I credit the "Deep Read" as the beginning of my story of how the Lord can move me and keep me stable all at the same time.

My spiritual journey really accelerated in 2011, as Pastor Jo gave me the keys to that transformative vehicle.

This has been one ride that has been too good not to share, and I'm excited about passing along the keys to the habit that has done so much to bring me renewal.

Renewal

When I'm feeling stuck
    And don't know how to start,
I need your precious fuel -
    I need renewal.

I'm so conflicted;
    My heart is divided.
To stop my inner duel –
    I need renewal.

Life is really hard;
    I struggle all the time.
Because the world is cruel –
    I need renewal.

So many times, Lord,
    I come to You in shame,
Feeling like such a fool –
    I need renewal.

I need to hear truth;
    I find it in Your Word.
To you I'm a jewel –
    You brought renewal.

Part 2

Preparing for the Journey

Chapter 9

Spiritual Nutrition

Renewal in any form rarely just "shows up." It typically comes through intentional actions that involve planning and preparation, as well as a new mindset.

It's important for those who follow Christ to understand that the Bible is to the soul what food is to the body. A responsive quiet time helps us get the optimal spiritual nutrition out of the Scriptures. Just as our physical bodies can experience renewal through an improved diet, renewal comes to our spiritual dimension when we improve how we feed it.

There are some New Testament passages that talk about milk and solid food as it pertains to biblical knowledge (1 Corinthians 3:1-3, Hebrews 5:11-14, and 1 Peter 2:2-3).

Think about the differences in how we intake liquids versus solid food.

Drinking liquids is typically a quicker process and

simply involves letting it enter our bodies. Liquids quench our thirst, and some even have nutritional benefits.

Intaking solid foods is a slower, more deliberate process. We use the act of chewing to process the food before we let it slide down our throat.

Listening to a sermon is like drinking liquids; most of us just pretty much take it in. A cursory reading of Bible verses is basically the same thing. Both are beneficial but require very little effort on our part.

A responsive quiet time is like ingesting solid food. It's a much more deliberate process that requires the effort to chew on God's Word, figuratively speaking.

> *Then he said to me: "Son of man, eat this scroll I am giving you and fill your stomach with it." So I ate it, and it tasted as sweet as honey in my mouth. Ezekiel 3:3*

Having a full stomach can be a pretty satisfying feeling. There's a greater sense of satisfaction when you've intentionally put some nutritionally beneficial food in your body. The same is true with the soul.

The opposite is also true, and I know how it feels to consume spiritually empty calories.

In his excellent book on Psalm 23, *The Lord Is My Shepherd*, pastor and author Robert J. Morgan reminds us, "We find nourishment by abiding in His Word, feeding on His faithfulness, and living on His promises."[1]

Morgan goes into great detail about sheep chewing their cud and relates it to Christians reading the Bible:

"Despite its distasteful nature, it's a perfect illustration of biblical meditation, which is a lost art among today's Christian believers. Meditation is the practice of chewing on a verse we've previously read, memorized, or studied until we digest it. It's the process of masticating a Scripture until it's broken down and assimilated throughout our souls. In this way, we become what we eat. We gain strength from nutrition.

> *"As a preacher, I'm amazed at how this works. I can study a passage – say, Psalm 23 – and read everything I can find about it while working at my desk. I can ferret out every commentary, check out every sermon, look up every word, and diagram every sentence. But the freshest insights come after I close my Bible ... My mind works on the verse the way my stomach works on the lunch I've eaten. ... This is the process of rumination. ... When applied to Bible study, this practice yields insights into the Scripture."* [2]

In John 15:7a, Jesus encouraged us this way: "Stay joined to me and let my teachings become part of you." (CEV) When I read this during one of my quiet times, it occurred to me that Christians need to ingest God's word to the point where it becomes an actual part of us. God's word should essentially become a vital organ in our body, so we can't maintain any quality of life without it.

The Bible is packed full of good stuff! We need to read it—and often—but go beyond reading so we really understand what it says and how it makes a difference in how we live. Connect with the words on an emotional and intellectual level. Once we get a taste of those fresh insights, we can't wait to dig in for more!

Jesus said in Matthew 5:6, "Blessed are those who hunger and thirst for righteousness, for they will be filled." I have sensed that hunger, experienced that thirst. But I rarely felt filled until I firmly took hold of Pastor Jo's advice and that "God Jobs" bookmark.

Chapter 10

Little Bookmark, Big Impact

It has often been said that "good things come in small packages," but I never imagined that a 2.875" x 8.5" bookmark would have such a big impact on my life. That unpretentious piece of paper gave me something I not only didn't know that I needed but also that I didn't know was possible.

Simply designed by Pastor Jo, the front of the bookmark has the heading "GOD JOBS" with the subtitle "Spiritual Disciplines for Thirsty Christians." It then features the quote from theology professor Robert Mulholland: "God Jobs are acts of loving obedience that we offer to God steadily and consistently to be used for whatever work God purposes to do in and through our lives."

According to Mulholland, there are three categories of disciplines, which are listed in order on the front of the bookmark:

The inward disciplines:
- Prayer–Fasting and praying Scripture
- Bible reading–Meditation/study

The outward disciplines:
- Simplicity – Live a simple life
- Solitude – Get alone with God
- Submission – Yield to others
- Service – Ministry to others

Together disciplines:
- Celebrate
- Confess
- Guidance
- Worship

I had never really thought of spiritual disciplines being categorized like that, but it really makes a lot of sense. Obviously, these categories aren't exclusive as listed; for example, service is an outward discipline but can also be a together discipline. But it was interesting to me to see how multi-faceted spiritual disciplines can be.

The back side of the bookmark has the information on "Bible reading and meditation: THE DEEP READ, using the Bible to connect with God."

The bookmark then outlines the five simple steps:
- First: Ask God to open the passage to you.
- Second: Ask God to give you a receptive/ open heart for what you read.
- Third: Read slowly in order to think more

about a word or phrase which has opened to
you.

- Fourth: If you feel led, use the phrase to form
  a prayer. Prayer lets us go beyond the letter
  of the phrase to experience how the Holy
  Spirit speaks to us through the words.
- Fifth: Don't rush. Relax and enjoy the experience. Let prayer move the words into your
  heart.

I have found it especially helpful to record the word
or phrase in a notebook. I usually refer to this as my
"journal," but for those who may have some anxiety
about that word, I can assure you that each entry
isn't at all lengthy, as most consider journal entries.

Over the years, my practice has developed into a
habit that works best in my life and the way I'm
wired. It may not be what connects for you, but we'll
touch a bit more on that later.

As I open my notebook to begin, I ask God to open
the passage to me. As I open my Bible, I ask God to
give me a receptive heart to what He wants me to
see. It's important to approach the Scriptures with
purpose but not an agenda.

I read the short passage, and if a word or phrase
doesn't "jump out at me," then I read it again, and
at least by the second reading, there's something
that gets my attention. (A friend with whom I once
shared this said she was surprised how reading the
passage a second time really helped something stand

out to her!)

In my notebook, I record the date, the passage, and what I call the "key" to the passage. I use the word "key" for a couple of reasons: one is for the sake of brevity, but mainly because it conveys the notion that a new treasure in the Scriptures has been unlocked for me. I then record my thoughts on the key. That leads to meditation and/or prayer, giving me the opportunity to "chew" on this truth that stood out to me.

That's what makes a "responsive" quiet time. Make whatever truth you glean from the passage portable; you can (and should!) take it with you. When you spend time praying and meditating on that key thought from Scripture, you're more likely to remember it throughout the day. It might even randomly pop into your head because the meditation process puts it into your head.

And this happens just by spending a few minutes with a few verses. It's really not complicated, either.

Here's an example, randomly selected from a time in which I was apparently reading through the Psalms using the New Living Translation:

6-27-15
Passage: Psalm 59:14-16
Key (v. 16): Each morning, I will sing with joy
Thoughts: I certainly do not do this, but I should. I need to claim joy in the morning and focus on God alone, not my burdens.

I typically use the New International Version for my reading and quiet time, but occasionally I'll switch to another translation for a while. That's a way to get a different perspective on some of those passages with which we tend to become familiar.

Another example, taken from a period in which I apparently felt the need to spell out the names of the months:

April 22, 2019
Passage: 1 Corinthians 5:6b-8
Key (v. 7): You may be a new … batch
Thoughts: New batch. Fresh. Different ingredients for different results. This is a new day – the old stuff may not work anymore. Live alive all day today in newness of life.

Many times, a single word gets my attention. It can be a very common word (I found one entry where the key was the word "some") or one with strong spiritual undertones (like "judgment," which was the key the day before "some").

Sometimes my Scripture reading is a single verse, but it still can make for a meaningful quiet time:

2-21-13
Passage: Galatians 6:10
Key: Opportunity
Thoughts: It's hard to see the window of opportunity if you keep the curtains closed. We have to be willing to look for the opportunities God gives us.

Sometimes, I choose to just record my prayer because that's my Spirit-led response:

Sept. 21, 2019
Passage: Jeremiah 16:14-21
Key (v. 19): Lord, my strength and my fortress
Thoughts: Lord, I do feel weak and under attack now – so much to do and so much contention. Rather than collapse and complain, may I run to you and remember that you are my strength and my fortress. I need you, God.

I have found that when I open my heart, what God reveals to me can come in any number of forms. It can lead to prayer or a song; it can lead me to think of something funny or clever; it can be sobering or humbling or something completely different. It's always fresh and never the same. That's probably why I've stuck with this practice for more than a decade!

I also think it might be what God would like for time with Him to be: fresh and memorable.

Remember, the idea is to truly find a key to unlock a truth that you can carry with you. Whatever becomes significant to you from the Scripture passage is something that should be thought through, prayed about, and meditated upon; that's how renewal occurs.

It's not just reading. It's not just jotting down a few words in a notebook. It's responding in a way that changes the way you think – about God, about yourself, or even about others. And did you notice how brief my thoughts were on each of the passages? A compact response is an impactful response.

You never know when a few verses can make a big impact on your life.

Chapter 11

Time With Him

One of the keys to a meaningful quiet time is approaching it as an opportunity to spend time with God. You're not just reading a book; you're reading a love letter from the Almighty One who created the universe, and love letters beg for a response from the recipient.

And that's the least we can do.

HOW we do that is up to each individual. God created us to be unique in every way, so there is not just one way to do a quiet time that is equally meaningful for everyone.

The internet is loaded with options. It may just be a matter of trial and error to find one that you can settle into because it fits you best. It's nice to have options, though, and from time to time, I'll actually use a different method, although the "Deep Read" is definitely my default setting.

More than 1,000 churches in America asked those attending to participate in a REVEAL survey to discover what helps Christians grow spiritually. Consistently over the years, the survey reflected the truth that "the most influential catalyst of spiritual growth is personal time spent in reflection on Scripture."[3]

I attended a church that participated in that REVEAL survey and was part of the committee charged with developing ways to encourage the congregation toward deeper spiritual maturity. Having a responsive quiet time was the foundation, so the committee would regularly host seminars to help explain the concepts.

As part of the seminar, a few tips were shared to keep in mind as you embark on your new path to spiritual maturity:

- Determine a regular time to spend time with God.
- Choose a designated place.
- Get the sleep you need – weary eyes and a foggy brain will interfere with your ability to get the most out of the time.
- Have a plan of where to read (more about this later).

No matter which method is used, it's important to start with a brief prayer to ask God to reveal what He wants you to know for that particular day.

Open your Bible and focus on those precious words.

I've already detailed the "Deep Read" method. There are some other methods that have been popular with those with whom I've shared this experience.

One is the "vowel" method: each vowel in the alphabet is used as a trigger for a potential response to the Scripture passage:

A - Ask questions (who, what, when, and where primarily; why and how are valuable questions which may prompt deeper study, but the others are better for the purpose of a quiet time)

E - Emphasize key words or phrases – what words stand out or are repeated (fairly similar to the "Deep Read")

I - In your own words (write a summary or paraphrase the text)

O - Other related Scriptures (note cross references or think of other places in the Bible that refer to and reinforce what you're reading)

U - Use what you've read (apply it to yourself; ask yourself how this truth will impact how you live)

With the vowel method, you select just one of the five vowels to use as the focus for meditation. I have found that it works best for me to decide which vowel fits after reading the Bible verses. The "Emphasize" option in the vowel method is similar to the

"Deep Read," but I have also utilized the other vowels in my quiet time.

Another option is referred to as the "SPECK" method; you examine the Scripture passage by asking a series of questions, each of which starts with the letters in the word "speck":

S – Is there a SIN to avoid?

P – Is there a PROMISE to claim?

E – Is there an EXAMPLE to follow or avoid?

C – Is there a COMMAND to obey?

K – Is there KNOWLEDGE about God to receive?

The SPECK method is popular with several people I know because it gives targeted things to search out. Others get hung up on it because they try to find answers to all five questions in a passage. That will rarely happen, so this is a good option for those who can accept that each reading will generally have at least one answer but could have as many as five.

Yet another option is referred to as "SOAP." (Some consider this to be a "clean" way to have a quiet time!) All four letters of this acronym combine to help you walk through the Bible passage:

S – Scripture (make note of the passage being

read)

O – Observation (what things do you notice going on in the passage?)

A – Application (how can this passage be applied to your life?)

P – Prayer (respond to God about what you read)

It's generally a good practice to have some sort of notebook to help record this information. It keeps you on track, plus people tend to remember things better if they actually write them down.

In terms of optional resources for a regular quiet time, one website that might be especially helpful is the Navigators ministry:

www.navigators.org

Chapter 12

Find Your Path

When I worked with small groups with a focus on spiritual development, we took time for what I call "devotion method exploration." Basically, between meetings, we would look at the same designated Scripture passages using one of the methods listed in the previous chapter.

This is a great exercise because it exposes you to each of the four methods over several days. By repetition, you get a better feel for how well you connect with each of them. You will find your path to renewal and greater spiritual growth when one of these methods seems to "click" with you. You'll just know when you're on the right path.

If you're new to having a regular quiet time, it's a good idea to set a goal for how often you plan to do one. It's not always feasible to plan on doing a quiet time seven days a week, but if that's your ideal, then make that your goal. If you're uncertain, start small by setting a goal of three to five days a week.

Once you've set that goal, make it more concrete by

setting specific days to do a quiet time. If your initial goal is three days, you might want to set aside time on Mondays, Wednesdays, and Fridays for that purpose. Some people whose lives are dictated by a calendar actually make themselves an "appointment" to do the quiet time.

Pick a specific place where you won't be bothered. Get organized in advance by placing your Bible, notebook, and writing instrument in the place you've selected. That way, when your "appointment" time comes, you're ready to go!

Making a commitment to this time, and to God, is what can make a huge difference in your spiritual journey.

In his book, *We Beheld His Glory*, author William Tinsley describes what his commitment to spending time with God looks like:

> *"Many years ago, I made it my habit to meet with Jesus in the morning at sunrise, outside. I started this on my patio in Texas. ... I continued this habit in Rochester, Minnesota on our deck overlooking the Mayo Clinic, and, most recently, under the aspen tree behind our house in Colorado. I have met him for prayer and devotion on cool Texas mornings before the heat rises. I have bundled up, scraped away the snow and ice and met him outside on frozen mornings in Minnesota and Colorado."*[4]

Can you imagine anyone going to such great lengths over the course of decades if it wasn't worth it?

In *The Lord Is My Shepherd*, Robert J. Morgan encourages believers to make an effort to spend time with

God regularly. He writes, "We have to learn to steal away for stillness. If you'll just give some serious thought to your life, you can figure out how to carve out a little zone of quiet each day for devotional meditation." [5]

In one of his Peanuts © comic strips set on the baseball field, Charles M. Schultz sets up the scene: a fly ball has been hit and is headed right toward Lucy. The ball drops on the ground about a foot from Lucy, who appears to just be staring ahead, obviously oblivious to the action of the game. As the manager, Charlie Brown is understandably upset and charges to the outfield to ask Lucy how she could have possibly missed such an easy ball to catch. Her explanation: "I was having my quiet time."

There's definitely an appropriate time and place for a quiet time! Just like the quiet time methods, it could take some trial and error to craft your perfect spot to meet with the Lord.

It may take some time to make this a habit, so don't get discouraged if you forget or if something interferes with your planned devotions. And if life just gets in the way (as it tends to do at times), don't beat yourself up for missing a quiet time "appointment." Give yourself grace for the moment and renew your commitment for your next quiet time.

The next section will be designated for devotion method exploration. The Scripture passages and format are provided to get you started. Please do all five quiet times for each devotion method to get a solid feel for how you connect with it.

Chapter 13

It's Time

I mentioned previously that music has contributed to my renewal. I'm thankful that God blessed some to write impactful song lyrics set to a variety of music styles and then provided talented singers to give voice to those songs.

When I was baptized at the age of 25, my pastor challenged me to take an interest in music designed to glorify God in my daily life and not just at church. He guided me to some local Christian radio stations to help me find one that I liked. In doing so, I found several artists whose voices and songs I enjoyed.

Wayne Watson is one such artist who had several contemporary Christian recordings in the 1980s, 1990s, and beyond. I have several of his CDs (having graduated from the original cassette tapes), have seen him in concert twice, and own a devotional book he wrote. It would be impossible for me to pick my favorite song of his, but I have developed a strong bond to one called "It's Time." Although I doubt it has ever been played on the radio, it's a meaningful song to me, and the message is as clear as the title: it's time to give your life to God and let

Him heal you and lead you.

When you do that, it's easier for renewal to come. It can be like a spiritual awakening.

> *"You are all children of the light and children of the day. We do not belong to the night or to the darkness. So then, let us not be like others, who are asleep, but let us be awake and sober." (1 Thessalonians 5:5-6)*

When I went to see Pastor Jo, I was at a point in my life where I couldn't see a lot of light, and my spiritual enthusiasm was slumbering. Maybe even hibernating.

Can you relate, either now or at some point in the past? Does it seem you're a little in the dark? Do you feel like your soul is in a deep sleep? Taking a little nap, perhaps? Maybe even it's just a little weary, so your spiritual eyelids are a tad heavy?

Awake! It's time!

For some, there comes a point when they know that the timing is right to do something to make a positive change. That moment certainly came when I made the decision to leave my abusive marriage. When I finally got really serious about losing weight and successfully achieved that, one of my friends asked me, "Why now?" I had to think about it for a moment, because there was really no specific thing that prompted the timing of something I had obviously needed to do for several years. So, my answer to him was simply, "It was just time."

Maybe you have been procrastinating for years about developing the habit of a regular quiet time with God, just as I procrastinated about losing weight. While both take effort, I can assure you that cultivating the quiet time habit is easier than losing a lot of weight! But each requires commitment and planning.

Your journey of spiritual maturity and renewal can have a new beginning like mine did. An open heart and an open Bible are the basics of what you need.

While I can personally vouch for this, I'm not alone in this discovery.

Prominent German pastor and theologian Dieterich Bonhoeffer had this to say about communication and closeness to God through the Scriptures: "Every day in which I do not penetrate more deeply into the knowledge of God's Word in Holy Scripture is a lost day for me." [6]

Wayne Watson and one of his sons, Adam, collaborated on a song called "Steal Me Away." The lyrics call out the need for us to spend time alone with God to be able to face the "devils and the dealers" in this world. "Could we maybe go somewhere and find some quiet time alone together, Jesus?"[7], the song proposes.

That's an offer Jesus will never refuse. All of the members of the Godhead welcome the opportunity to bring you renewal.

God's Word is truly the foundation for spiritual growth. Hearing biblically-based sermons is good, but it's not enough. Reading the Bible is an important habit of every Christian, but it's not enough. Maturity and renewal happen when we go beyond hearing and reading. We must personally respond to the Scriptures.

> *Jesus answered, "It is written: 'Man shall not live on bread alone, but on every word that comes from the mouth of God.'" Matthew 4:4*

> *(Jesus) replied, "Blessed rather are those who hear the word of God and obey it." Luke 11:28*

> *Do not merely listen to the word, and so deceive yourselves. Do what it says. ... whoever looks intently into the perfect law that gives freedom, and continues in it – they will be blessed in what they do." James 1:22, 25*

> *Then he opened their minds so they could understand the Scriptures. Luke 24:45*

> *What we have received is not the spirit of the world, but the Spirit who is from God, so that we may understand what God has freely given us. 1 Corinthians 2:12*

A responsive quiet time has its basis in these Scripture passages and others. We see in the above verses that the Holy Spirit helps us understand what we read so we can obey it, act on it, and be blessed by it.

The ways we are blessed by this practice are numerous, which is why renewal is inevitable and why I get so enthused about helping others find the same fulfillment in their quiet times as I have!

Part of my excitement stems from the fact that it's really pretty simple and doesn't have to take a huge chunk of time. But it does take discipline—especially at first—and commitment. It's actually not a lot when we consider the commitment the Lord has made to us. You may remember that "For God so loved the world that he gave his one and only Son, that whoever believes in him shall not perish but have eternal life" (John 3:16). I consider that to be a pretty substantial commitment from the Lord to me!

Approach this regular "appointment" as the perfect opportunity to fellowship with God. Keeping that kind of company gives us the short-term, immediate benefits of daily insight and direction.

We learn more about God and living the Christian life because His words have been written down so we can remember them better and refer back to them. I have learned that if I need more than three things from the grocery store, I have to make a list, either on paper or in my phone. Putting things in writing helps refresh my memory of what I need and allows me to refer back to that list as I cruise around the store.

Reading Scripture and having a quiet time isn't about making lists of things we should and shouldn't do, however. Remember that the Bible is God's love letter to us, the way He best communicates to us, in hopes we'll respond.

Think of it this way: the Bible is God's primary means of communicating with us. That makes the Scriptures the logical launching point for our communication with Him.

The more we read the Bible, the more we know about God, and the more He is able to reveal Himself to us so we can live out His will for our lives.

In her devotional book, *Keeping It Brief, Volume 1,* author Cheryl Phillip-Jordan put it this way: "Why should He reveal Himself to us when we refuse to spend meaningful time with Him, when we treat Him as a spare tire, as a hotel bellhop, or as a first aid kit?"8

We are cheating ourselves when we treat God in those ways because our Creator and Almighty Lord has so much to offer us. One reliable way we receive His blessings is through the communication provided in the Bible.

At its best, communication involves honesty and depth in a setting that ignores busy schedules and excludes external influences. What happens when two individuals have this type of meaningful communication between themselves? They grow closer together.

There's no one who's better to get close to than God.

As the years go by, I find this to be true, whether living alone or with others. Sticking close to God provides unmatched security and comfort.

> *"Come near to God and he will come near to you."*
> *James 4:8a*

In my mind's eye, in the depth of my soul, I have crawled into my Father's lap to be held and consoled. It has provided a place of comfort where tears can fall freely onto the chest of the One who created me and knows me better than anyone.

I have shared a candlelight dinner with God. This intimate setting allowed me to talk aloud about the troubling and perplexing things in my life, with the full knowledge that He heard me and was there with me.

God tucks me into bed at night, just as a parent would a child. As I pull the covers around my neck, I hug myself and squeeze my arms, smiling because I know God uses that to show me His love. Sometimes I talk to the Lord about a thing or two that happened that day, thanking Him for something, mentioning some specific situation, or confessing where I fell short. I sense His loving response to whatever it may be. Every night, I "hear" God telling me that He loves me, calling me names of endearment: dear child, precious child, even "Princess." That "God hug" helps me peacefully enter sleep knowing how much God loves me, because I have grown so close to Him.

If you want that kind of relationship with the Lord, then it's time to experience the renewal that comes from a responsive quiet time.

> *"Who is he who will devote himself to be close to me?" declares the Lord. Jeremiah 30:21*

Are you that person who is ready to devote yourself to being close to the Lord? Open heart, open Bible. Let's go!

"Just a Closer Walk With Thee"

I am weak but Thou art strong
Jesus keep me from all wrong
I'll be satisfied as long
As I walk, let me walk close to Thee
Just a closer walk with Thee
Grant it, Jesus, is my plea

Daily walking close to Thee

Let it be, dear Lord, let it be

When my feeble life is o'er

Time for me will be no more

Guide me gently, safely o'er

To Thy kingdom's shore, to Thy shore

Just a closer walk with Thee

Grant it, Jesus, is my plea

Daily walking close to Thee

Let it be, dear Lord, let it be

Part 3

The Beginning of Your Journey

Chapter 14

Exploration: SPECK

Refresher: the SPECK method gives you five questions for things to look for in the designated passage. It's not uncommon to find more than one question answered, but it's rare to find all five. Just look for what's there and don't push it trying to find something that isn't there.

DATE:

READING: *Exodus 40:34-38*

S in to avoid?

P romise to claim?

E xample to follow?

C ommand to obey?

K nowledge about God to receive?

DATE:

READING: *Psalm 100:1-5*

S in to avoid?

P romise to claim?

E xample to follow?

C ommand to obey?

K nowledge about God to receive?

READING: *Matthew 12:30-32*

S in to avoid?

P romise to claim?

E xample to follow?

C ommand to obey?

K nowledge about God to receive?

DATE:

READING: *Philippians 4:4-7*

S in to avoid?

P romise to claim?

E xample to follow?

C ommand to obey?

K nowledge about God to receive?

DATE:

READING: *Hebrews 12:18-24*

S in to avoid?

P romise to claim?

E xample to follow?

C ommand to obey?

K nowledge about God to receive?

After completing all five quiet times, consider how insightful this method proved to be for you. If desired, write your impressions of SPECK below.

_____

_____

_____

_____

_____

_____

_____

_____

_____

_____

_____

_____

Chapter 15

Exploration: Vowels (AEIOU)

Refresher: the vowel method gives you the opportunity to respond to the passage based on things to search out using the first letter of one of the five vowels. After reading the verses, decide which of the five makes the most sense to use for your response.

DATE:

READING: *Deuteronomy 1:29-31*

A sk Questions:

E mphasize Key Words:

I n Other Words:

O ther Verses:

U You! Application:

DATE:

READING: *Isaiah 43:18-19*

A sk Questions:

E mphasize Key Words:

I n Other Words:

O ther Verses:

U You! Application:

DATE:

READING: *Jeremiah 15:19-21*

A sk Questions:

E mphasize Key Words:

I n Other Words:

O ther Verses:

U You! Application:

DATE:

READING: *Acts 19:11-16*

A sk Questions:

E mphasize Key Words:

I n Other Words:

O ther Verses:

U You! Application:

DATE:

READING: *1 Peter 1:13-16*

A sk Questions:

E mphasize Key Words:

I n Other Words:

O ther Verses:

U You! Application:

After completing all five quiet times, consider how insightful this method proved to be for you. If desired, write your impressions of AEIOU below.

_____

_____

_____

_____

_____

_____

_____

_____

_____

_____

_____

_____

_____

Chapter 16

Exploration: SOAP

Refresher: the SOAP method gives you the
structure for a quiet time.

S cripture: *2 Chronicles 29:3-6*

O bservation:

A pplication:

P rayer:

DATE:

S cripture: *Lamentations 3:19-24*

O bservation:

A pplication:

P rayer:

S cripture: *Haggai 2:6-9*

O bservation:

A pplication:

P rayer:

DATE:

S cripture: *Luke 12:49-53*

O bservation:

A pplication:

P rayer:

S cripture: *2 Corinthians 1:8-11*

O bservation:

A pplication:

P rayer:

After completing all five quiet times, consider how insightful this method proved to be for you.
If desired, write your impressions of SOAP below.

_____

_____

_____

_____

_____

_____

_____

_____

_____

_____

_____

_____

_____

Chapter 17

Exploration: Deep Read

Refresher: the "Deep Read" method has you focus on a word or phrase that jumps out at you, then encourages reflection and meditation on the significance of it.

DATE:

Passage: *Ecclesiastes 5:1-3*

Key Word or Phrase:

Reflections/Thoughts:

DATE:

Passage: *Habbakuk 1:2-5*

Key Word or Phrase:

Reflections/Thoughts:

DATE:

Passage: *Romans 12:1-2*

Key Word or Phrase:

Reflections/Thoughts:

DATE:

Passage: *1 Timothy 4:1-5*

Key Word or Phrase:

Reflections/Thoughts:

DATE:

Passage: *Revelation 6:9-11*

Key Word or Phrase:

Reflections/Thoughts:

After completing all five quiet times, consider how insightful this method proved to be for you. If desired, write your impressions of the "Deep Read" below.

_____

_____

_____

_____

_____

_____

_____

_____

_____

_____

_____

_____

Chapter 18

Additional Readings

As I have guided others on starting a responsive quiet time, the most frequently asked question is: "How do I pick what to read?"

I have often had the benefit of Sunday school lesson books which include passages to read each day, but not everyone has that same advantage.

If you use any type of devotion book, there are hopefully some Bible references you can pull out to use for your quiet time. I would recommend noting the Scripture and doing your own quiet time before reading the prepared devotion so your response is more influenced by the Holy Spirit than the devotion writer.

There are reading plans galore in Bibles, in apps for your smartphone, or on the internet. If those recommended passages seem too long, pare them down to just a few verses. When time is limited, facing a reading that encompasses several verses can be overwhelming and frustrating and may discourage you from doing a quiet time.

It's good to read large passages of Scripture, but for the purposes of a responsive quiet time appointment, it's easier to find a key when your focus is on a limited number of words.

A concordance can guide you to a handful of different passages on a particular topic that might interest you, so you can utilize those for your quiet time. Another option is to select a book from the Bible and go right through it.

At one point, I felt drawn to the book of Jeremiah. I never seemed to be able to enthusiastically latch onto a prepared study of that book. After a few years of being frustrated by that, I decided to dedicate my quiet time to reading that prophetic book. I would read a few verses until I felt compelled to stop and respond.

I'll admit that I did start and stop a few times, as other materials seemed timely, but I continued to return to Jeremiah. With 52 chapters, it certainly took a while! I don't regret the extended commitment, however. At the conclusion, I took the time to go back through all of my journal entries and wrote out some of the most significant things I found in the book of Jeremiah.

Lots of options for quiet time readings, but where to start? Because I know how difficult that can be, I've made up some lists that can be used. The readings in each list aren't necessarily connected, but they are organized. (I even included a section for my favorite prophet, Jeremiah!)

They're not in any particular order, and you can feel free to mix and match. Use your preferred quiet time method (or mix and match those as the Spirit leads) and be consistent in your time with the Lord.

Psalms

Psalm 1:1-3
Psalm 13:2-6
Psalm 18:30-32
Psalm 36:7-9
Psalm 40:4-8
Psalm 60:11-12
Psalm 82:1-5
Psalm 98:1-3
Psalm 131:1-3
Psalm 145:14-16

Gospels

Matthew 5:14-16
Matthew 8:5-10
Mark 5:18-20
Mark 9:30-32
Mark 14:34-36
Luke 6:37-42
Luke 10:39-42
John 8:28-30
John 13:31-35
John 16:31-33

Jeremiah

Jeremiah 1:7-9
Jeremiah 6:16-19
Jeremiah 9:23-24
Jeremiah 10:23-24
Jeremiah 16:10-12
Jeremiah 30:10-11
Jeremiah 32:37-41
Jeremiah 42:5-6
Jeremiah 50:33-34
Jeremiah 51:11-14

50/50 Mix (Old/ New Testament)

Exodus 6:1-5
Joshua 4:21-24
2 Samuel 22:26-31
Isaiah 6:1-8
Daniel 7:13-14
Acts 5:12-16
Romans 8:38-39
Colossians 2:9-10
1 Peter 1:17-21
Revelation 11:16-19

Chapter 19

Extended Version

Sometimes musicians will record an extended version of a song. That version is rarely played on the radio but is typically made longer by adding an instrumental solo to the song as a way of highlighting the musical ability of the recording artist or group. It provides an enhanced experience but isn't the typical version.

There's actually an "extended version" of a quiet time that has also proved very enlightening to me.

I was introduced to this method a few years ago at Christmas time. I have continued the practice and have found it to be an excellent way to get a much-needed fresh perspective on the very familiar but very meaningful "Christmas story" during the Advent season. I've begun sharing it with others—developing a reading schedule with a specific theme—and have received some positive feedback.

This method of doing devotions is a variation of an ancient spiritual practice known as *Lectio Divina* (divine reading).

For these devotions, I recommend setting aside 30 to 45 minutes for one day each week (or as it seems fitting based on what you're searching out in the Bible). Part of the reason is that the length of the passages is typically more verses than is recommended for the daily quiet time.

Go to a place where you can have quiet and won't be interrupted; feel free to put a note on a closed door if that's what it takes! Being able to focus is key.

As with all devotion methods, begin with prayer, asking God to reveal something fresh and new to you.

It's a good idea to have paper or an electronic device to record your reflections, just as with the regular responsive quiet time. Start by reading the passage, but don't rush through it. Make note of any words or phrases that stand out to you.

This all sounds pretty familiar so far, but the *Lectio Divina* asks you to do more in order to get more out of the passage.

As you read, imagine yourself in the situation. If the passage centers around a particular person, put yourself in their place. Close your eyes and immerse yourself in the story. What do you think your surroundings might be like? What is your emotional and mental response to what's going on? What questions come to mind that may not be recorded in the Scriptures? (My imagination ran rampant when all of the Advent devotions centered around angelic visits!)

Feel free to interact with the passage in your own unique manner. Making yourself part of the story will help you experience the passage in a fresh way. Let your thoughts flow freely onto the page as you connect deeply with the words of Scripture.

Spend time meditating on the passage and all of your reactions to it. Is there a message directly for you? Pray whatever is revealed to you, and if you don't feel the Spirit give you a message, pray anyway – and respond to God's word.

Reading the passages about the birth of Jesus reminds us of the importance of obedience to God, even when nothing seems to make sense. But there are so many other things we pick up when we immerse ourselves in the passage.

For example, when reading about the angel's visit to Zechariah announcing that his completely barren wife, Elizabeth, was going to have a baby in her old age, I gained perspective on many things. One was how fitting it is to acknowledge, just as Elizabeth did, that "the Lord has done this for me" (Luke 1:25).

After spending my *Lectio Divina* time with this passage, I had a situation pending which was causing me some anxiety. I had been released from the hospital a couple of weeks prior, and some good friends wanted us to go to a special Christmas event in a town a little over an hour away. I was still very weak and wasn't sure how well I could tolerate the drive, let alone constantly walking the few blocks in the center of town where all the events would occur.

The day before we were supposed to go, our friends decided to check out a different Christmas activity on their own. I was greatly relieved, as God had answered my prayer about how to handle the situation, and I was able to praise Him by declaring, "The Lord has done this for me." My takeaway was that many times, our role is to pray, worship, and wait.

A related feature for those who are visual people is to include the practice of *Visio Divina* (divine seeing) when appropriate. For the "Angelic Advent" devotion package I put together, I encouraged people to use a picture, ornament, or other type of image of an angel.

I also suggested they feel free to conclude their time with one of the Christmas songs about angels. Because so many songs have their basis in Scripture, it's totally appropriate to include music as part of the "extended version" of your responsive quiet time.

So that you can give *Lectio Divina* a try, the reading schedule for the "Angelic Advent" theme follows. Note that there are five weeks of readings; it's fine to start early or extend your time beyond Dec. 25th!

First Week of Advent – Luke 1:11-25
Second Week of Advent – Luke 1:26-38
Third Week of Advent – Matthew 1:18-25
Fourth Week of Advent – Luke 2:8-20
Fifth Week of Advent – Matthew 2:13-15, 19-23

Chapter 20

Habit Forming

If you Google something like "how many days it takes to form a habit," there's a good chance you will get this result from Healthline.com: "It can take anywhere from 18 to 254 days for a person to form a new habit and an average of 66 days for a new behavior to become automatic."

If you did the 20 exercises to "test drive" the four options for a responsive quiet time, you're well on your way to developing this habit to bring renewal to your spiritual life!

I cannot stress enough that the key to renewal is based on an openness to hear from the Lord during these times. We are so quick to react as soon as we hear or read something; that's not what this is about.

It's so important to take time to listen to the Holy Spirit conveying the message found in that particular Scripture passage. Even if it's just a brief moment, pause. Don't try to rush the process by reading the Bible with a writing instrument in hand, ready to jot down the first thing that comes to mind.

Listen.

Mother Teresa, with her busy lifestyle helping the poorest of the poor in Calcutta, India, as a missionary, understood the importance.

"Listen in silence," she wrote in *No Greater Love*, "because if your heart is full of other things you cannot hear the voice of God." [9]

After all, it IS called a quiet time.

The saint continued, "But when you have listened to the voice of God in the stillness of your heart, then your heart is filled with God." [10]

What do you think your heart is filled with right now? Is it filled with God?

Renewal is a process, and God is constantly at work in our lives if we open ourselves to allowing Him to – ouch! – change us. He will if we will.

I don't know that my heart was ever filled with God until I began doing a responsive quiet time. I'm not greatly inspired or overwhelmed with amazing insights each time I meet with God. But I don't really get that sense of being filled with God unless I practice this habit that has joyfully formed in my life.

That's because spending this time with my Heavenly Father has brought me to a place where I don't just know about Him – I know Him.

It's the best habit I've ever formed. But I confess that I don't give God enough praise for using it to bring renewal to my life.

As I was writing this book, one of my quiet time readings landed me in 1 Chronicles 29, where a prayer of David is recorded in verses 10-13. These verses are a fitting prayer of praise for the way God works in our lives.

> *Praise be to you, LORD, the God of our father Israel, from everlasting to everlasting. Yours, LORD, is the greatness and the power and the glory and the majesty and the splendor, for everything in heaven and earth is yours. Yours, LORD, is the kingdom; you are exalted as head over all. Wealth and honor come from you; you are the ruler of all things. In your hands are strength and power to exalt and give strength to all. Now, our God, we give you thanks, and praise your glorious name."*

Amen.

Heart Notes

My heart knows there are far more acknowledgments than I will list here, but out of gratefulness, I will mention some who contributed in various ways.

Vicky Pannella is completely indispensable to me as a creative soundboard. Her cover photo selection was impeccable, and she helped me think through many key points of the book. I can't imagine doing a big writing project without her. And the only thing I can say about Heather Lipe of Woodchuck Arts is: "WOW!!"

God is always the inspiration behind my writings, and He is always so faithful to show me "amazing things." During the process of writing "Renewal," I sensed the need for a different spiritual home, although I couldn't define what I needed. My renewal came as the Lord led me to a great church. I have not only been inspired and challenged by the biblical teachings of Pastor Jeremy, but some new friends came with the package. I am especially thankful for fellow introvert Donna, who faithfully prayed me over a major obstacle in writing this book, despite not knowing what "project" was a struggle for me. I asked; Donna prayed, God delivered.

My ever-faithful pair of besties, Valerie and Rex, are

always there for me through everything. Rex gave me some much-needed information to help "that one paragraph" make sense. Likewise, my sister Beverly Smith (author of The Silver City Bank Robbery and her poetry collection, Keeping It Simple) gave me a great suggestion for wording when I wasn't happy with my original thoughts. My prayer partner, Sharron, constantly helps me process life. Dear friend Bob provides me with regular snippets of humor and doses of encouragement – he may need to be initiated into the Encouragers Hall of Fame with Doug Apple!

Of course, my husband, Dave, has accepted the task of putting up with me, my projects, and my accompanying moods. God certainly blessed me greatly as I was "on the move."

Foot Notes

[1] Robert J. Morgan, *The Lord Is My Shepherd* (Howard Books, 2013), p. 59.

[2] Morgan, pp. 59-60

[3] Cally Parkinson, *"How REVEAL's Top Churches Deliver Spiritual Growth,"* (Willow Creek Association, 2020)

[4] William Tinsley, *We Beheld His Glory* (The Tinsley Center, 2021), Preface

[5] Morgan, pp. 60-61

[6] Dieterich Bonhoeffer, *Meditating on the Word* (Cowley Publications, 1986), p. 2.

[7] Wayne Watson and Adam Watson, *"Steal Me Away,"* Living Room (Material Music, 2002)

[8] Cheryl Phillip-Jordan, Keeping It Brief, Volume 1, *Short Daily Devotions to Draw You Closer to God* (Dove Christian Publishers, 2021) p. 106

[9] Mother Teresa, *No Greater Love* (New World Library, 2001), p. 3.

[10] Mother Teresa, p. 3.

About the Author

Sharon Merz is a life-long Midwesterner who has always been drawn to the written word. Readers can connect with her on her Facebook page, "Sharon Merz, Author." She can also be reached by email at livingdevo@outlook.com. "Renewal" is her second book.

Printed in the USA
CPSIA information can be obtained
at www.ICGtesting.com
JSHW012028270923
49135JS00016B/150